CRADLEY HEATH, OLD HILL & DISTRICT

A SECOND SELECTION

RON MOSS

First published in 2004 by
Sutton Publishing

Reprinted in 2013 by
The History Press
The Mill, Brimscombe Port,
Stroud, Gloucestershire, GL5 2QG
www.thehistorypress.co.uk

Title page photograph: Making chain by hand.
The chainmaker is connecting a length of
chain to a hook. Cradley Heath and the
surrounding district was world famous for
its wrought-iron, handmade chain of all
sizes. (*Ron Moss*)

British Library Cataloguing in Publication Data
A catalogue record for this book is available from the
British Library.

ISBN 978-0-7509-2497-9

Typeset in 10.5/13.5 Photina.
Typesetting and origination by
Sutton Publishing Limited.
Printed and bound in Great Britain by
Marston Book Services Limited, Didcot

The Old Tudor Haden Hall, home of the Haden family for many hundreds of years, awaiting
restoration. (*BCS Collection*)

CONTENTS

THE BLACK COUNTRY SOCIETY

The Black Country Society is proud to be associated with Sutton Publishing of Stroud. In 1994 the society was invited by Sutton Publishing to collaborate in what has proved to be a highly successful publishing partnership, namely the extension of the *Britain in Old Photographs* series into the Black Country.

In this joint venture the Black Country Society has played an important role in establishing and developing a major contribution to the region's photographic archives by encouraging society members to compile books of photographs of the area or town in which they live.

The first book in the Black Country series was *Wednesbury in Old Photographs* by Ian Bott, launched by Lord Archer of Sandwell in November 1994. Since then 55 Black Country titles have been published. The total number of photographs contained in these books is in excess of 11,000, suggesting that the whole collection is probably the largest regional photographic survey of its type in any part of the country to date.

This voluntary society, affiliated to the Civic Trust, was founded in 1967 as a reaction to the trends of the late 1950s and early '60s. This was a time when the reorganisation of local government was seen as a threat to the identity of individual communities and when, in the name of progress and modernisation, the industrial heritage of the Black Country was in danger of being swept away.

The general aims of the society are to stimulate interest in the past, present and future of the Black Country, and to secure at regional and national levels an accurate understanding and portrayal of what constitutes the Black Country and, wherever possible, to encourage and facilitate the preservation of the Black Country's heritage.

The society, which now has over 2,500 members worldwide, organises a yearly programme of activities. There are six venues in the Black Country where evening meetings are held on a monthly basis from September to April. In the summer months, there are fortnightly guided evening walks in the Black Country and its green borderland, and there is also a full programme of excursions further afield by car. Details of all these activities are to be found on the society's website, www.blackcountrysociety.co.uk, and in *The Blackcountryman*, the quarterly magazine that is distributed to all members.

PO Box 71 · Kingswinford · West Midlands DY6 9YN

INTRODUCTION

The area covered by this book is almost identical to the area referred to as the centre of the chainmaking trade of the Black Country. This area, measuring around 2.4 × 2.8 miles, included the towns of Netherton, Quarry Bank, Old Hill, Cradley and Cradley Heath. Figures gleaned from a Home Office survey in 1911, at a time when the manufacture of small chain by hand was still quite substantial and had yet to be affected by the invention of electrically welded steel chain in 1901, shows that out of 939 chain workshops in England and Wales, 918 were to be found in the area just defined. At that time the towns of Old Hill and Cradley Heath were located in the old county of Staffordshire and the other three were to be found on the border of Worcestershire. Today the towns of Old Hill and Cradley Heath come under the Metropolitan Borough Council of Sandwell while Netherton (the lower ton or town to Dudley), Quarry Bank and Cradley are in the Metropolitan Borough Council of Dudley. In each case the dividing boundary line was either the River Stour or one of its tributaries.

The River Stour and its many brooks and streams were very important before the coming of the steam engine late in the eighteenth century. They provided the water power for the many mills along their length which milled the corn and worked the forges and slitting mills that produced the iron to service the many iron-using trades in the local area. In the early days the slit iron rods were used by the nailmakers, thousands of men, women and children who sweated away making nails usually for very little reward. When machine-made nails started to be produced in nearby Birmingham in the 1830s, the poor nailers could not keep pace with the quantity made or the price that they were produced for.

By this time, following Henry Cort's invention of grooved rolls in 1783, round iron was being produced in such places as Cradley Forge and Rolling Mills and the nailers adapted their hearths and tools in their backyard forges to enable them to make small chain by hand. From around 1800 many chain firms were being established in the area although a lot of the small chain remained a domestic industry, many families making chain as 'outworkers' for larger firms. This trade started to decline between the two world wars although some lingered on until the 1950s, with the last one laying down her hammer in 1973.

Noah Hingley, who in the early nineteenth century was a manufacturer of small chain in Newtown, Cradley Heath, brought prosperity to the area when he manufactured the first large cable chain in 1820 for a Liverpool shipowner. The area became world famous for its chain industry and also many other ships' fittings including anchors and shackles. In 1928 Mr Percy Jump, a director of Noah Hingley of Netherton, when addressing a meeting of the Staffordshire Iron & Steel Institute was proudly able to tell them that there were 6,000 employed in the chain trade in the district and that they were producing 90 per cent of the total chain that was manufactured in the British Isles at that time.

The Cutting of the Canals

The Black Country, having no navigable rivers on its plateau, cried out for a good transport system that would allow its industrialists to move their minerals and finished articles about the area. This came in 1768 when the first canal was opened from Wednesbury to Birmingham. The nearest canal to serve the Old Hill and Cradley Heath area was the Dudley No. 2 canal, which wound around the contours of Netherton Hill at 453 ft above sea level and was opened in 1798. It did not reach Cradley Heath but was able to serve such places as Doultons glazed fireclay works whose products, made from the excellent fireclay obtained from their quarry in the Saltwells coppice, was delivered by boat to the works. It also served many other brickworks set up along its route and several ironworks including Noah Hingley's works at Bishton's Bridge, Netherton, and his Old Hill ironworks in Powke Lane. Further along it provided transport for the large Coombs Wood tubeworks before passing through the Lapal tunnel to join the canal from Birmingham at Selly Oak.

Railways

Many collieries and works that were located below the level of the canal were connected to it by a series of tramways. An early rail link was referred to locally as 'The Horse Tramway', which served the large Corngreaves ironworks of the British Iron Company (later the New British Iron Company) and provided a connection to the canal basin on the Dudley No. 2 canal close to Bishton's Bridge, above Saltwells Road. It passed through the area that was later to become the site of the Old Hill (Spinners End) goods yard and then passed under the Upper High Street at Reddal Hill near the present Cradley Heath library and provided the reason for the nearby public house opposite the library to be named the Bridge Inn. With the later availability of steam engines the rails were then rerouted to cross Lawrence Lane, Halesowen Road and Wrights Lane, on their way to the canal basins near Garratts Lane bridge opposite the site of the Old Hill gasworks in Powke Lane.

The mainline railway came to serve the area when the line was opened by the Stourbridge Railway Company (later the GWR) from Stourbridge to Cradley Heath on 1 April 1863, with a goods branch to Cradley colliery and the Corngreaves works. On 1 January 1866 the line was extended to Old Hill and, with the cutting of the tunnel under the Rowley Hills, the line was opened to Galton Junction at Smethwick, so providing a connection with the Wolverhampton to Birmingham line.

On 1 March 1878 the line was opened from Dudley (South), later known as Blowers Green, to Old Hill with an intermediate station at Windmill End. On the same date a line was opened from Old Hill to Halesowen station making Old Hill an important junction. On 10 March 1879 the Withymoor basin branch was opened forming a canal/rail/road interchange with the Dudley No. 2 canal.

In September 1905 three more halts were opened on the Dudley to Old Hill line, namely, Old Hill (High Street), Darby End and Baptist End. On 1 August 1907 the Spinners End branch was opened to goods only, leading to the establishment of the goods yard at Spinners End connecting the track to the main line just outside Cradley Heath station. In the past few years, the depression in the land occupied by this goods yard was slowly infilled, compacted and piled and has been developed for residential bungalows.

Trams
Public road transport in the area was provided by horse buses until the coming of the electric tram. The Dudley–Old Hill–Cradley Heath route was officially opened on 19 October 1900; this operation ended on 31 December 1929. A branch line from Old Hill running to Blackheath via Waterfall Lane (The Tump) was opened on 19 November 1904 and closed on 30 June 1927. The nearest tram route towards Cradley came from Stourbridge via the Lye, and was extended to The Hayes (the parish border line) on 1 November 1902.

Buses
The motor buses that followed the trams were mainly operated by the Midland Red company, together with a few small operators who provided an excellent service for all the towns covered by this book.

Education
Education in the form of charity schools came early in the area with one being established at Reddal Hill in 1790. The vast ironworks complex at Corngreaves, run by the New British Iron Company, provided a school for workers' children in *c.* 1848–9. This is still in use in Plant Street, Old Hill, today.

Religion
Parish churches were established in the second half of the nineteenth century at Old Hill and Cradley Heath, while many chapels of every denomination were to be found among workers' housing in most streets.

'Thirst after Righteousness'
Almost every street and road boasted up to half a dozen public houses; these were needed to quench the thirst of the manual workers in iron-making and iron-using trades. Furthermore, markets and shopping centres provided good food at a reasonable price, as they still do today.

How Old Hill got its Name
Many interesting historical facts can be obtained by researching the origin of place-

names. It is fascinating to discover how a road or a place, be it a hamlet, town, city or county, obtained its name. Many places are named after exceptional features that are connected with it or near where it is situated. Some are quite ancient and it is difficult to find documentary proof to confirm their identity. Two well-established local towns are a good example: Dudley is said to be named after the ancient local ruler, Dudda, it was his 'ley' or lands, while Cradley is said to be named after Creda or Cruda. A number of books tell us that the name Rowley describes the terrain in the area, 'rough ley' – barren and treeless. Travellers would use the paths across these high grounds in preference to the wooded valleys on each side, which could hide wild animals or footpads. Brierley Hill was described as high ground (climbing up from Stourbridge) covered in briars, and early nineteenth-century maps show it to be mainly an open gorse-covered common criss-crossed with paths. Some areas adopt names associated with local features such as the Saltwells, which took the name from a brine bath that was established in the woods after a well was sunk and a brine spring was discovered. These salts had healing qualities, similar to Woodhall Spa in Lincolnshire, that soothed aching joints and muscles. The Earl of Dudley and his family used the bath, causing a stir when they arrived in their carriages. Local football teams, such as West Bromwich Albion and Aston Villa, also found it beneficial. The well still exists and contains the same healing salts but about 50 per cent weaker; this was confirmed by a survey carried out by the Black Country Society's Industrial Archaeology Group in 1975 (see IA Studies No. 1).

Just below the Rowley Hills, on the sheltered south slope, one of the Lords of the Manor built himself a house constructed of bricks. *Magna Britannia* records the fact that Thomas Grey and Roger Somery 'did build themselves brick houses as their seats'. What is so special about that, you might say, but at that time bricks were just reappearing after a gap of around a thousand years. No bricks had been made since the Romans left the British Isles around the second century and the few that were made were very rare and of course expensive, and could only be afforded in the fourteenth century by well-off men such as the Lord of the Manor. Other dwellings in the district would be constructed of wood, mud and stones, especially the locally available 'Rowley Rag', which is still quarried today on the Rowley Hills. During research a map dated 1796 showing the extent of the Brickhouse Farm and Estate, which at that time was owned by St John's chapel, Deritend, was found to contain a large area in the centre owned by Lord Ward and known as 'The Ruddings'. This was probably the site of his manor. The road running down the left-hand side, known today as Doulton Road (formerly Dog Kennel Lane), is shown as Rudding Lane and it states that the lord maintains a right of way from this lane to the centre plot. From that day to this the area is still known as the Brickhouse Estate.

A similar phenomenon occurs at Pensnett, where in the past only a local landowner or industrialist was able to afford the equally rare clay tiles to roof his house when most people used thatch or wood. This was also thought to be so unusual that 'The Tiled House' appears on early maps, and one of the roads in the area today still bears the name Tiled House Lane.

Haden Hill was named after the de le Haueden family, later shortened to Haden, who were the Lords of the Manor, the lands given to them after the Norman Conquest, while Corngreaves is said to be derived from coney greaves, a rabbit warren on the bank of the River Stour. My grandfather, a miner and ironworker, hailed from Woodside near Holly Hall. An early address that I came across while researching census returns some years ago gave his address as 'By the Woodside'; it appears that the Saltwells Woods, a couple of miles further down the road, at that time reached as far as the present Dudley to Brierley Hill railway line, the first two words being dropped over the years.

Having lived in Old Hill for the past forty years I have always been fascinated by the origin of its name. The town, which is shown on a map that was drawn by Joseph Brown in 1682 and was included in Robert Plot's book, the *Natural History of Staffordshire* published in 1686, is certainly not on a hill. In fact when J. Wilson Jones, the Cradley Heath librarian, wrote his book on the *History of the Black Country* he convinced his readers that the name was originally 'Old Dell' and that this had been misspelt over the years as it was passed from mouth to mouth. J.W. Jones came to Rowley Regis from Walthamstow in 1921; he said that he came to rejoin his family who he claimed had lived in Rowley since 1642. At the time that he wrote his book there was very little written about the Black Country and every local historian began their research by reading his book.

The name 'Old Dell' appeared to be quite plausible because if you stood on Old Hill Cross, once a staggered crossroads, now a large traffic island, whichever direction you wished to travel in, whether it be 'up to Dudley', 'up to Rowley', 'up to Haden Hill' or even 'up to Cradley Heath' (after crossing a small depression where once there was a ford and where the brook is now culverted under Brook Lane), you had to climb out of a hollow. It fooled me for a number of years until my colleague Edward Chitham told me that while he was researching for his book on the Black Country he managed to make contact with Jim Jones who, after a brief conversation, finally admitted that he had made up the name. So how did Old Hill become so named?

I was carrying out some research many years ago in the Salt Library, Stafford, looking at their very good collection of old trade directories and making notes of the various traders that had businesses in Old Hill. These directories list the names of the person followed by their trade and then their address in the town. Shortly after starting I came across one whose address was recorded as 'Halesowen Road, OLD HALL'; I thought it must be a spelling mistake. I then found several others and on returning home and looking at photocopies I came to the conclusion that this was one of the possibilities of the naming of Old Hill. It was another case of the town being called after the nearest well-known landmark; very useful when giving directions as there has been a hall (Haden Hall) on the hill nearby for the past 600 years. From evidence found in its cellars the present Tudor hall is said to stand on the foundations of a much earlier building. Early travellers could have been told to meet someone in the town or village 'near the old hall', which, like previous examples quoted, eventually became shortened to 'Old Hall'.

Ron Moss, January 2004

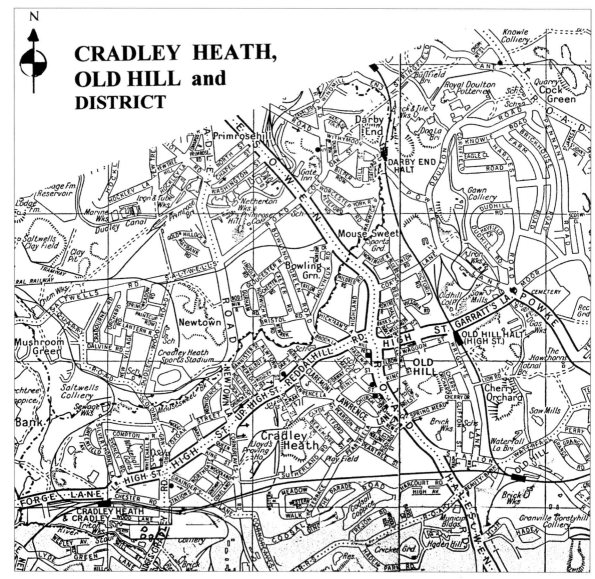

N

CRADLEY HEATH, OLD HILL and DISTRICT

This page from an old West Midlands street atlas, dating from around the 1950s, is very useful because it shows the Earl of Dudley's Pensnett mineral railway, disused by the 1950s, just entering the district from the left-hand side of the map. Some of his collieries and also the old GWR branch line running out of Old Hill, which closed in 1968, can also be seen. Most of the location areas of the photographs contained in this book can be traced on this street map, apart from Corngreaves Hall which is located to the south of Barrs Road (bottom centre). The famous Cradley furnace and forge on the River Stour was located just below the word *FORGE*, next to Cradley Heath & Cradley railway station. Fragments of the New British Iron Company's Corngreaves Railway can be seen leaving the works (bottom centre) and also crossing the Spinners End goods branch just above the words CRADLEY HEATH on its way to the Dudley No. 2 Canal.

1

Transport

Old Hill, 'Labour Club' stop. Midland Red LD8 no. 4044 pulls in to pick up passengers on its way to Dudley. Although the main road has been re-aligned, the position of this bus stop has remained the same. (*Ron Moss*)

Chara outing. This is probably a Bible class outing from the Macefields Mission, Old Hill, c. 1920. The charabanc, a Burford (a joint USA/UK firm), was obtained by Samuel Johnson, 'Supreme' Ltd of Stourbridge, in 1920. Samuel Johnson was born in King Street, Old Hill, in 1879. The photograph was loaned by Ms Jennifer Walker of Old Hill, who tells us that her step-grandfather is the gentleman in the dark overcoat and trilby hat above the word 'Stourbridge'. (*Collection of Ms J. Walker*)

High Street, Cradley Heath, 16 May 1959. Many of the shops are still in evidence today, but used for different purposes. The Midland Red GD6 Guy double-decker, fleet no. 3563 has almost finished its journey from Wednesbury to Cradley Heath, via Great Bridge and Dudley on the 244 route. (*Ron Moss*)

Chester Road, Cradley Heath, 1968. All these buildings by Cradley Heath railway station have since been demolished. The Vine & Railway Inn is no more; its site is now a corner garden. The original 1863 railway station buildings disappeared with the modernisation of the station in 1983, and the boiler erection towers of Cradley Boiler Company no longer silhouette the skyline. Even the Midland Red D9-type bus, which is waiting to start its 244 run to Wednesbury via Great Bridge, can only be seen today in a museum or on the preserved rally field. (*Sandwell Archives, Smethwick*)

The floods in Old Hill. During 1968 and 1969 Old Hill suffered some heavy downfalls of rain, and on this occasion the only vehicles able to get through the flooded Halesowen Road were heavy lorries and buses. Here a Midland Red D9-type bus, probably on the 243 route from Dudley, creates a bow wave as it passes the Victoria pub on the left. A lot of the property on the right-hand side of the road has now been demolished. The light-coloured cottage standing out in the centre background is thought to be quite old, dating back to the days when a toll-gate existed around Cox's Lane. (*Ron Moss*)

Old Hill Cross, 11 April 1964. Plenty of onlookers have paused, while out shopping in Old Hill, to watch the skills of this Scammell tractor driver and the Pickfords crew struggle to get a large tracked earth-moving vehicle past the bollards. In the lower photograph the Midland Red Inspector makes his way on to the scene to arrange for his 238 service bus to negotiate the area on the wrong side of the road. The 'Rhubarb Chapel' and its neighbouring buildings in the upper photograph have now been replaced by a large traffic island, but the buildings in the lower view are still there although the Dudley Co-op has changed hands. (*Ron Moss*)

Unusual bus working in Old Hill, 19 January 1969. This Midland Red D9-type bus (fleet no. 5427, EHA427D) has been forced to run 'off-route' owing to roadworks on the main Cradley Heath to Old Hill road. It is a rare sighting of a bus travelling down Trinity Street, Old Hill, on the 138 route, Kingswinford (Mount Pleasant Inn) to Birmingham. The large building in the background is the Trinity Street Schools. (*Ron Moss*)

The Midland Red bus garage in Forge Lane, Cradley Heath, viewed from the site of the former Great Western Railway goods yard in 1971. The buildings of the goods yard were demolished a few years ago. The intermediate sets that were used by horse-drawn vehicles and, later, three-wheel Scammells and trailers can still be seen. On the garage forecourt sits an S23-type Midland Red service bus, the last single decker to be designed by the company. Through the left-hand doorway some of their double decker fleet (probably DD12 Daimler Fleetlines) are parked, while behind the centre doorway are some stored touring coaches. (*John Pizzey*)

The Old Hill to Dudley railway branch line crossed Garratt's Lane by means of this cast-iron bridge. This December 1969 view looks down Old Hill High Street (later named Highgate Street) and clearly shows the limited clearance of 12ft, with Wright's Lane coming from the left. A railway halt was located close to the bridge. (*Ron Moss*)

'A bridge too low.' On 28 February 1970 a lorry driver misjudged the height of his vehicle and rammed it halfway under this bridge. As the railway that passed over it had been closed to passengers since 15 June 1964, and to goods traffic since 1 January 1968, the decision was taken to remove the bridge. This took place between 6 and 18 October 1970. (*Ron Moss*)

Old Hill station signal-box, 26 May 1957. This spanned both the Down platform from Birmingham to Stourbridge Junction and the platform that was used for trains to Halesowen and Longbridge. The public service on the Halesowen line ceased on 5 December 1927, but trains continued to carry workers to the Austin works at Longbridge until their withdrawal in 1958. (*Ron Moss*)

Old Hill station, 26 May 1957. This station sign, also repeated on the Down platform, clearly shows that, in its early years, Old Hill was once a very busy junction with two branches leaving the station, one on each side. Even in 1957 it had nineteen staff (including one parcels van driver) to man the station in shifts; by 1972 this had been reduced to two. (*Ron Moss*)

The interior of Old Hill signal-box, showing the large number of levers necessary to control this once busy railway junction. Several bells and instruments can be seen on the shelf but several more have been removed as the branch lines have been closed. These signal-boxes were always immaculately kept. (*Ron Moss*)

Signalman Peter Robins keeps a close eye on a passing train, ready to return the signal lever to 'danger' to protect its rear as soon as the train has passed his signal-box. Peter was one of the last signalmen to operate this box before it was taken out of the system. It was a tradition that the levers were always pulled with a duster in the hand. (*Ron Moss*)

Old Hill railway station on 27 August 1963, showing the Halesowen branch line which left the main Birmingham to Stourbridge line just above the water-tank in the centre of the picture. The track being removed served the platform on the left, which was used by workmen's trains to the Austin works at Longbridge until they ceased on 1 September 1958. This whole area is now covered by trees. The lower photograph shows the outside of the original station building, on 1 September 1963. The Midland Red D7 bus is providing a special alternative service while trackwork is replaced, while a Stanier 2–8–0 engine is on duty on the line to the right. The building was demolished after the disastrous fire on 13 September 1967. (*Ron Moss*)

Cox's Lane level-crossing, 1 November 1958. 'The Dudley Dodger' (as the rail service from Old Hill to Dudley was known) is being driven from the cab of the auto-coach number W160 towards Dudley, with 0–6–0 pannier tank no. 6418 supplying the power. A Midland Red single decker waits for the signalman to open the gates, the signal-box being hidden by steam. Since the railway closed this area has been covered by industrial buildings. (*Ron Moss*)

Old Hill station, 30 May 1959. An SLS (Stephenson Locomotive Society) special train, hauled by an ancient MR 2F 0–6–0 engine no. 58271, is taking the Halesowen branch line on a 'Tour of the Birmingham Area'. The signalman is standing level with his box ready to hand the firearm of the engine the 'tablet' that authorises him to use the single line safely to Halesowen. The photograph is taken from the old 'Austin' platform, with Palmer's timber yard visible on the right. (*Ron Moss*)

Cox's Lane level-crossing, showing the small, neat, typical GWR signal-box that protected the road crossing over the Old Hill to Dudley railway line, *c.* 1968. This line carried goods traffic and small local passenger trains, usually consisting of either a steam engine fitted out for auto-train working (push-pull) and a single coach, or a GWR diesel railcar. The line was a victim of the Dr Beeching cuts and was closed to passenger traffic on 15 June 1964 and goods traffic by early 1968. By August 1968 the track had been completely lifted. (*Ron Moss*)

Darby End halt. The disused railway halt at Darby End has lost its name signs in this 1969 dramatic view. The concrete structure did not serve the railway passengers for very long after it had replaced the original wooden halt in 1957. Gawne Lane twists drunkenly underneath the line and, shortly after the line's closure, no time was lost in lifting the track and removing the bridge so that the lane could be straightened out. Unfortunately this allowed vehicles using the lane to travel much faster and a speed camera has now been installed to try to restrict the traffic to 30mph. (*John Pizzey*)

GWR railcars. In the 1950s the Old Hill to Dudley branch rail service was often handled by one of these AEC-engined railcars. There were thirty-eight members of the class: the above photograph shows No. 15 being serviced on shed; below, with a slight difference in body design, is No. 22. (*Ron Moss*)

Old Hill (High Street) halt after it had lost its trackwork, 10 May 1970. This was situated on the Old Hill Junction to Dudley branch line, which opened to passenger traffic on 1 March 1878 and was closed to passengers on 15 June 1964. The old housing and pubs, on the left of the photograph, have been cleared and new houses now occupy the site of the halt. (*Ron Moss*)

Railway relics. Ron Moss with the type of name signs that were seen on the local railways around thirty years ago. The 'Old Hill' sign came from the station on the Stourbridge to Birmingham main line and is appropriately fitted to a GWR cast-iron lamp standard that once stood on the same station platform. The 'Old Hill (High Street) Halt' sign was in use on the branch line between Old Hill and Dudley until it was closed by the Beeching axe on 15 June 1964. (*Cheryl Aston*)

Fresh vegetables were still being delivered by horse-drawn vehicle to householders in Dalvine Road, Dudley Wood, in April 1957. Children have always been fascinated by animals, and this little girl's grandad is making sure that she gets a good look at a way of life that will soon be passing into history. The horse is also making sure that the photographer records his best side. (*Ron Moss*)

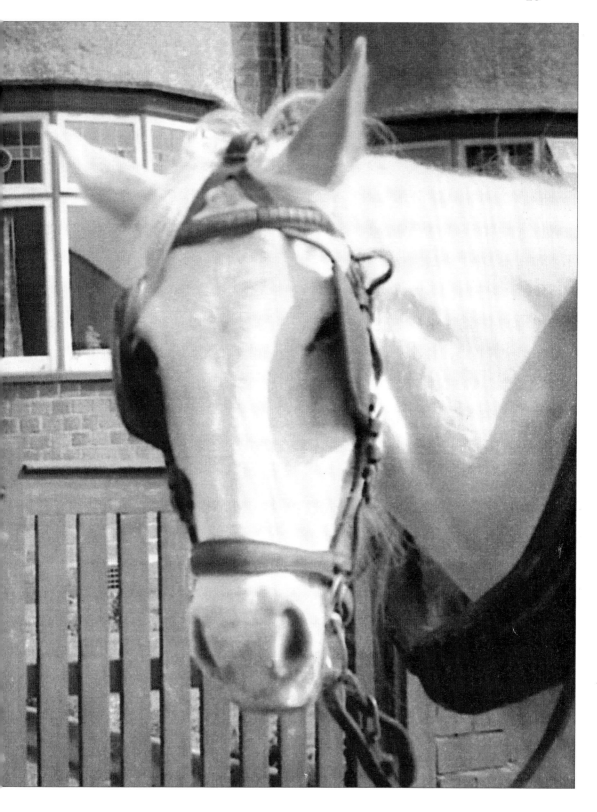

The horse-drawn greengrocer's cart in Dalvine Road, Dudley Wood. (*Ron Moss*)

The horse-drawn narrow boat. For many years, until the later adoption of an engine, this was the motive power used to propel boats along the canal system. Here, this old method of bringing a boat up through a set of locks has caused a crowd of interested spectators to gather. (*Ron Moss*)

Cobb's engine house. This is the area around Cobb's before restoration began in February 1973. In the foreground is an old working boat, details of which from my notebook are as follows: *Judith Ann*, Steven & Keay, Oldbury and Walsall, 5522870; perhaps these details might interest canal enthusiasts. Since this photograph was taken much has been done to improve the appearance of the area, including a very good interpretation centre on the right-hand towpath that was opened in 1998 to celebrate the opening of this Dudley No. 2 canal 200 years ago. (*Ron Moss*)

2

Street Scenes

Christ Church, Cradley Heath, still complete with its surrounding walls, ornamental fencing and bushes, May 1970. In the background is the Anchor Hotel where many chainmakers gathered on pay day to be given their share of a chainmaking gang's earnings for the week by the chainsmith who led the gang. Needless to say a portion of their wages never left the pub. Note the old-style traffic lights. (*Ron Moss*)

Cradley Road, Cradley Heath, *c.* 1915. The two buildings on the right, Samuel Tibbetts the high-class butcher and the famous Cross Guns Inn, are still there today albeit trading in different items. Below them stand rows of cottages behind which could be found small chainshops. The site today is occupied by the Majestic cinema building, which unfortunately, after a spell as a bingo hall, has closed its doors to the public. On the left the

barber's shop still carries on the same trade, but the tram tracks and cobbled sets have long since gone. The horse-drawn carts and horse deposits are now a thing of the past. The coaches of a vintage train rumble over the bridge at the bottom of the road while the schoolchildren put on a classic 'clothes of the day' show for us. (*Sandwell Community Library Archives*)

High Street, Cradley Heath, summer 1975: looking up the High Street, with the Five Ways Inn (Charlie Wright's) on the left and the long-established businesses of Burtons the tailors, Marsh & Baxter, the butchers, and Woolworths on the right sandwiching the Central Market Hall with its curved roof. An ex-Midland Red double decker DD12 bus, probably on the 243 service to Dudley, is shown in West Midland Passenger Transport Executive livery. The town would be losing most of these well-known High Street shops within the next few years, but A. Griffiths's renowned watch and jeweller's business is still in the same position in 2003. (*Peter Barnsley*)

High Street, Cradley Heath, summer 1975: looking down the High Street, with the new development of the Cradley Heath market area visible on the bottom left, while new tall bank buildings have appeared on the right-hand side. The Leyland National bus on the 138 service to Birmingham appears to be in the blue and cream livery of the West Midland Passenger Transport Executive which took over some of the services in the area in December 1973. (*Peter Barnsley*)

Cradley Heath, looking towards the Five Ways, early 1960s. This view of the High Street did not change for many years. Although most of the shops have since changed hands, the most significant alterations have occurred to the business on the right, the Cradley Heath Motor Company Ltd. (This is now of course the Moon Under the Water pub, which opened in May 1997.) For many years motor vehicles were serviced and sold from the garage, which was owned by a member of the famous Henn family, the local jewellers who were responsible for providing wedding rings for many Black Country marriages. Sometime in the mid-1970s it was converted into Vernons supermarket, and then a Kwik Save supermarket, followed by a firm that sold electrical goods, furniture and lawnmowers, finally becoming the public house. Two other long-established firms shown below the Cradley Heath Motor Company are Brooks Bros, the greengrocers and fruiterers, and of course Holden's the shoe shop, now the Cheltenham & Gloucester Building Society in the Louvre building. The Midland Red Omnibus Company is represented by the LS18-type single decker bus at the stop in the High Street. (*Sandwell Community Library Archives*)

Cradley Heath looking towards the Four Ways, early 1960s. In this view of the High Street from the zebra crossing, still in the same position today, looking up towards the Four Ways, the Midland Red provides public transport for shoppers, with a single decker coming into the town (possibly on the 238) while a D5 double decker bus (MHA 533) heads up to Dudley on the 243. The Mobil garage sign of the Cradley Heath Motor Company can just be deciphered in front of the double decker. A three-wheeled Scammell railway lorry and trailer, probably from Cradley Heath station goods yard (now the site of the bus station and car park), has just driven over the zebra crossing. (*Sandwell Community Library Archives*)

Cradley Heath High Street, November 1967. Local shoppers will recognise many of the names above the shops which made Cradley Heath a famous shopping town and have long since gone. The photograph is remarkable because of the lack of traffic – imagine trying to stroll across the road like that gentleman in the dark suit. Incidentally, near the spot where he is about to cross was the centre of the subsidence in February 1914, the most damage being caused around the location of the Talbot Hotel, known locally as the 'Big Lamp'; this was on account of the large lamp that was fitted between the top two upstairs windows. The fixing bracket boss can be seen here, and is still there today, but Broadmead, the electrical appliance dealer, has long since gone. (*Ron Moss*)

Holden's shoe shop in the Louvre building and Brooks Bros, for many years the vegetable and fruit vendors in the town, can be seen here. Next door to Brooks Bros it is just possible to make out the 'V' of Vernons supermarket, which of course is now occupied by the Moon Under the Water pub. How Cradley Heath has changed. (*Ron Moss*)

Old Housing, Bannister Street. This 1974 photograph shows the mix of housing and chainshops that made up this street, named after the early chainworks that was located down below on the left in the Newtown district of Cradley Heath. Note the Staffordshire blue paviours, limestone sets and 'Rowley Rag' gutter-edging that make up the footpath on the right-hand side of the street, typical materials used in the Black Country. Today these are either removed or covered over. (*Ron Moss*)

Congreaves Road in the early 1970s, looking towards the Four Ways a few years before the bulldozer began its work of destruction. The Four Ways Inn (the Manchester) can still be seen in the distance opposite Barclays Bank building. The inn is no longer there and the bank is now the office of SAS, an accountancy firm. (*Ron Moss*)

The top end of Cokeland Place, Cradley Heath. This scene, looking towards the junction with Congreaves Road, shows substantially built workers' housing with fully grown trees much in evidence. The road is said to be named to commemorate the fact that in the early nineteenth century the Congreaves works of the New British Iron Company used this area to convert the coal to coke in preparation for its use in their blast furnaces. (*John Pizzey*)

The lower end of Cokeland Place, at the junction with Graingers Lane, 1971. Behind the first house can be seen a typical works yard of a small engineering firm backing on to the railway embankment. (*John Pizzey*)

'Where's the station?' The strangely named Station Road, Cradley Heath, as it appeared in 1971. The original Cradley Heath railway station was situated several hundred yards away in Chester Road, and even this has no been replaced by a modern station in Forge Lane. A variety of housing is shown in this view, which has since been replaced by industrial buildings. The two famous old chainmaking firms of Richard Sykes and Connops were located on the opposite side of the road. (*John Pizzey*)

Housing variety, June 1971. This view, looking down St Anne's Road from the Five Ways, Cradley Heath, is a good example of the variety of house styles that were often found in a Black Country road, starting with a portion of the iron fencing surrounding the Witley Memorial church and ending with the café on the corner of Compton Road. The first building is a classic corner shop, selling confectionery, tobacco, household goods and food, and a house built as a pair. Next door there are two obviously older dwellings that might have been 'pit-pulled' by the nearby Whitehall colliery. A much grander building stands alongside which for a time served as a doctors' surgery, accommodating medical staff that moved up from Cradley Road when their surgery became a training centre, which had been established earlier in Providence Street in Newtown. The team of doctors was able to move back again when their new surgery was built on the opposite side of Cradley Road. To keep the memory alive this new surgery contains examples of stained glass taken from doors and windows in this grand building. The remaining houses are typical Victorian dwellings. Sadly every house in this row has gone. (*John Pizzey*)

St Luke's Sunday School on the corner of Newtown Lane and School Street, Cradley Heath. Since its original use for education it has been used by many organisations including the Boy Scout and Girl Guide troops. A popular attraction in the mid-twentieth century was the ballroom dancing held every Thursday evening, when people of all ages danced to the latest gramophone records beneath a rotating 'mirror ball'. (*John Pizzey*)

Houses in Newtown Lane. Built on a sloping site, these houses once stood below St Luke's Sunday School in Newtown Lane. Looking at the height of the central doorways compared with the windows, these were probably 'entries' running to the rear of the houses where the actual doors into them were found. On the extreme left is the beginning of Bannister Street and the Holly Bush pub, the only building that can still be seen today. (*John Pizzey*)

Victorian workers' housing. Hollybush Street, Cradley Heath, does not appear today on the current A–Z maps apart from a small stretch, a few yards long, connected to Upper High Street, which will soon be wiped out by the proposed Cradley Heath bypass. The remainder of the road vanished with the new housing developments of the late 1970s. This view shows the bottom part nearest to the Holly Bush pub and is a good example of Victorian workers' housing development. 'Rowley Rag' sets and kerbs edge the road. (*John Pizzey*)

Industry combined with housing. Hollybush Street near the Baptist Mission, 1971. The double-entry opening, two houses further up, signifies a small business at the back of the houses, probably a chainshop, while a little way on can be seen a fairly large garage. In between, the two larger front windows could have supplied the area as small shops when first built. From the Mission upwards, the housing was all cleared in the late 1970s. (*John Pizzey*)

Today everyone refers to this supermarket in Cradley Heath as Kwik Save (or the Quickie) but this photograph shows the building in its early days when it was occupied by Fine Fare. All the prices are pre-decimalisation. A packet of tea has been reduced from 1*s* 9*d* to 1*s* 4*d*, while 8oz of Nescafé has been reduced from 8*s* to 4*s* 2*d*. The buildings on the right have since been replaced by several new smart shops. (*Dunn's Imaging Group PLC*)

This interior photograph of the Fine Fare supermarket shows more examples of pre-decimal prices, with bacon joints priced at 2*s* 4*d* per lb. The presence of balloons suggests that this is probably a pre-opening photograph. (*Dunn's Imaging Group PLC*)

Cradley Heath's large market closed in 1967 for redevelopment and this photograph dramatically shows the building of the new, present-day market. The old entrance (next to the gas showroom) is still visible. Further on is the nursery school in Grainger's Lane and further on still are Grainger's Lane Methodist church and Sunday school, the latter having been demolished and replaced by a car park in the last year or so. Above the church can be seen Cradley St Peter's church and Homer Hill, Cradley. (*Dunn's Imaging Group PLC*)

An evening shot of the Woolworth store in the High Street, Cradley Heath. Today these premises are occupied by Iceland, the freezer centre and general store. The original Woolworth store with its '3d and 6d stores' sign (3 penny and 6 penny articles on sale) over the entrance doors was a familiar sight from at least the mid-1930s. Next door on the right is the long-established shop of J. Biggs, Confectionery and Tobacco, another familiar sight for many years in the town. The ownership has since changed hands but they sell the same goods plus, of course, National Lottery tickets. (*Dunn's Imaging Group PLC*)

Clifton Street, Old Hill, viewed from the Cherry Orchard end of the street in 1969. These neat rows of Victorian houses have all been swept away and replaced by a modern development. In the distance at the end of the street and standing in Station Road is the front of the Ebenezer Strict Baptist chapel, whose datestones indicate that they were laid in September 1903. This chapel is still in regular use and well maintained. (*John Pizzey*)

Clifton Street, Old Hill, 1969. This view from the Station Road end shows little change to the buildings on the right, but beyond the trees above the car the Victorian dwellings have been cleared wholesale on both sides of the street and replaced by new housing. The 'gas-tarred' end of the terrace housing on the left has been replaced by a Sandwell MBC neighbourhood office. (*John Pizzey*)

Nos 94–100 Cherry Orchard, 1966. This photograph looks down Cherry Orchard (north side) towards Wright's Lane, which can be seen passing along the bottom of the road. All around this area there were the forges and workshops of James Potts & Sons Ltd, manufacturers of a great range of spades and edge tools. This firm ceased production at the end of 1969 and the buildings were knocked down in May 1970. All the housing in the area was demolished by August 1970. (*W.C. Frise*)

No. 95 Cherry Orchard, 22 February 1970. This house, located to the rear of nos 94–100, was approached through the gap or entry which can be seen below the first two houses. Immediately behind the house was the embankment that once carried the track of the Congreaves railway on its way to the nearby canal basins on the Dudley No. 2 canal. (*Ron Moss*)

Halesowen Road, looking towards Old Hill and about 300 yards along the Netherton side of Old Hill Cross, 17 December 1972. Every building shown here has since been demolished. The shop on the right-hand side, with the signs outside, is where Ivan's fish and chip shop was probably first established before moving to the much larger premises on the corner of Lawrence Lane and Reddal Hill Road. The next house along from Ivan's is quite a substantial, detached residence, with a centre door and walled front garden. (*Ron Moss*)

Halesowen Road, looking towards Old Hill Cross, which can just be seen in the distance, 17 December 1972. Apart from a few buildings most of these late nineteenth-century houses have been demolished and replaced. (*Ron Moss*)

The ever-changing face of Old Hill, 2 April 1970. This view shows the approach into Old Hill town from Netherton along Halesowen Road. The shop of D.M. Smith on the left was famous for many years when it was known as Verrecchia's, a purveyor of fine ice-cream. The two shops alongside replaced a pair of long-standing advertisement hoardings. The yard entrance beyond the next two shops led to one of the many blacksmith's shops found in the area that supplied oddwork (small pieces of ironwork such as shelf brackets, pipes and hooks, see page 73) to many trades. All this side of the road was swept away during road-widening work in the early 1990s. (*Ron Moss*)

Highgate Street (formerly High Street), Old Hill, could still boast that it had two water pumps located on the pavement on 10 May 1970. This one was situated between Pott's newsagent's shop and house no. 81. The railway bridge can just be seen in the top left of the picture. (*Ron Moss*)

Pit-pulled. Even after the Second World War many examples of buildings that had been affected by subsidence, owing to the mining of coal, ironstone and clay, could be found in the Black Country. Recorded in September 1974 when it was still occupied, this example, located in Dudley Road, was one of the last to be demolished. (*Ron Moss*)

Old Hill Cross, looking down Reddal Hill Road, 1969. The single-storey building on the left has had a very chequered history, almost as chequered as the bottom half of the butchers shop in the centre of the row. The right-hand portion, occupied by the two shops at the turn of the century, is said to have formed the waiting room for the trams from Dudley and Blackheath to Cradley Heath. When the trams ceased operating on 31 December 1929 two shops were formed. The centre shop was then occupied by several butchers, the first being John Goodwin, then Ken Beard followed by Tony Hewitt and, until the lease expired in 1972, Ray Nicklin. Lloyds Bank, which occupies the left-hand portion in the photograph then took over the right-hand portion, while the other shop was occupied by A.C. Kendrick & Son Ltd, seed merchants and animal feeds who were next door to Mrs Witcherley and her wool shop. In the background can be seen the houses in Hill Passage awaiting the arrival of the bulldozer. (*John Pizzey*)

Highgate Street, Old Hill (originally High Street before Old Hill and Cradley Heath were merged into one address for postal reasons in 1967), 17 December 1974. The prominent double shop supplied the needs of local families before the coming of the supermarket. Known locally as Beattie's, it was alway well stocked and spotlessly clean. Beattie would jot down your grocery bill on a small piece of cardboard and then reckon it up with great accuracy in pounds, shillings and pence. The double entry on the left of the shops led to several houses around the rear yard. These were demolished before the Second World War, one of the reasons being that because the backs of the houses were built against the wall they had no safety rear exit. Several families from here were rehoused in Victoria Road, Old Hill. (*Ron Moss*)

The corner shop, Boxing Day 1969. This is no longer a corner shop; the houses on the right-hand side of the road remain but the Duke of William pub, standing out below them, has been demolished together with everything on the left, the large building being the Tabernacle chapel. (*Ron Moss*)

This 1972 photograph of Best Street, Old Hill, shows its neat rows of Victorian dwellings, providing homes for many ironworkers and miners employed within walking distance of the houses. The corner shop is visible and at least another two shops were located down this typical Black Country street. It was probably named after Benjamin Best, who was the agent for the New British Iron Company at Corngreaves. He married Emilene Georgina Barrs. One of their daughters, Emilene Mary, married Walter Bassano, and their son, George Alfred Haden-Best, built Haden Hill House which has since been restored. (*John Pizzey*)

Dudley Street, Old Hill, 2 April 1970. The left-hand side of the street, showing the salon of Dianne, Hair Stylist, and six houses, before they were all swept away by the road developments in 1987 and the building of Apsley House in about 1988 near Old Hill Cross. The road in the foreground is Ash Street which was originally named Bank Street. (*Ron Moss*)

The manse. 'A house provided for a religious minister' is the dictionary description of a manse. This substantial house located in Dudley Street, Old Hill, bore the datestone to say that it had been built in 1879 and was recorded around a hundred years later. In 1987 the whole street was demolished and the sheltered accommodation of Apsley House now occupies the area. (*Ron Moss*)

How on earth was this 1970s photograph taken of busy Old Hill Cross, with not a soul in sight? On the left, the chemist Bellamy & Wakefield has been replaced by Verns, while Ye Olde Cross Inn next door has now vanished together with the Royal Exchange (known to locals as the Glasshouse because of its large glass windows) almost opposite. On the extreme right, just visible, is the always neat and tidy menswear shop of S. Barden, once a coffee house. (*Ron Moss*)

In this 1971 view a shaft of sunlight cuts across the one-way part of Elbow Street that comes up from Halesowen Road and the main shopping area of Old Hill. The row of four houses on the left were later demolished to make way for the expanding works of Thomas B. Wellings Ltd (their office building can be seen halfway down the street, on the left beyond the houses). Just a glimpse is included on the right-hand side of the Kings Head pub which was to close the following year. T.B. Wellings finally ceased production in 2001 and their factories are now being replaced by a Barratts housing development. (*John Pizzey*)

Church Street, Old Hill, 1971: an example of workers' housing with the Precision Patterns works based at its junction with Lawrence Lane. The supporting wall of the Corngreaves railway embankment is just visible on the extreme left. (*John Pizzey*)

Lawrence Lane, Old Hill, shown in 1971, is one of the few byways to be shown on the old 1820 parish map. Here it is joined on the right by Claremont Street which is indicated by dotted lines on the 1882/4 OS map. Some of the vanished industry can still be seen, with the Everite tool factory on the left, and, located at the junction, one of the many chainworks of the district. The houses shown in the centre of Lawrence Lane are still there today, although at the turn of the twentieth century they were the homes of factory owners and businessmen in the district, whose names and addresses appearing in business directories. Claremont Street has also retained the houses shown, while industry on the corner site has been replaced by new housing. (*John Pizzey*)

The Reddal Hill end of Lawrence Lane, Old Hill, with Plant Street branching off to the left, 1971. Hidden behind the row of cottages on the left were brewhouse chainshops where women laboured during the day making small chain. All the houses shown here were demolished in the late 1970s and early 1980s and replaced with sheltered accommodation by Sandwell MBC. (*John Pizzey*)

A Black Country lane. This 1969 view of Moor Lane, which runs from the traffic island on Powke Lane, Old Hill, and follows a twisting route to join Ross and Siviters Lane, Rowley, shows little change today with regard to the restricted width of the lane and the hedgerows, but the house in the upper centre was demolished long ago leaving a few brick remains as a reminder of where it stood for many years. Some history books describe this as being the main stagecoach route to Rowley, with passengers being asked to leave the coach and walk because of the steepness of the lane. Funeral cortèges also had to use this route from Old Hill to Rowley before the churches in Old Hill and Cradley Heath were built. (*John Pizzey*)

Originally these two fine houses with their central doors were probably built to provide homes for two gentlemen industrialists and their families. However, in this 1971 photograph they were being used as offices for Eric Bagley (Steels) Ltd and Horseley Metals. Their location is on the corner of Lawrence Lane where Plant Street heads off towards the Corngreaves schools. Halfway down Plant Street on the left can be seen the remains of one of the notorious chainshops where women are recorded, in 1859, as 'working like slaves' for a pittance, by a visiting chain union delegation from the north. (*John Pizzey*)

Looking out from Codsall coppice over Harcourt and Codsall Roads at the construction of the Riddings Mound flats in the 1960s, with the Rowley Hills making a superb backdrop to the scene. These particular flats were dramatically demolished using explosives a few years ago. Trejon Road starts its ascent in the bottom right of the picture. (*Dunn's Imaging Group PLC*)

This is an action shot of Bonson's stall at Cradley Heath old market in the corner of the indoor market, which served the area from 1922 until its demolition in 1967, just after this photograph was taken, to make way for redevelopment including a new market hall. This popular stall sold crockery, table and glassware, and figurines, providing retirement and birthday presents for the local population. (*Peter Barnsley*)

Looking towards Cradley Heath from St Peter's, 1959. Many of the prominent buildings that make up this view from St Peter's church tower, Cradley, have now disappeared. The Stourbridge to Birmingham railway line cuts across the picture towards the top, while below it the vast tract of waste ground of Porters Field is now occupied by the large industrial estate. A line of trucks awaits collection on the siding that dipped down on the right to pass under the main line and serve the Spinners End goods yard. Very noticeable middle left is a rare view of the long gone Cradley Heath gasworks, while a little nearer is the bottom yard of the Jones & Lloyd chainworks. A couple of houses can be seen next to the Jolly Collier Inn in the centre of the picture and another two isolated homesteads are visible a little further to the right. Many buildings in the foreground have now vanished. (*Collection of Peter Barnsley*)

3

Inns & Public Houses

The Gate Hangs Well at the junction of Cole Street and Oak Street, where the
corrugated iron shop was located. The pub, complete with a mounted gate,
is probably named after a toll-gate that guarded the junction of these two roads
many years ago. (*Ron Moss*)

The Corngreaves Hotel at the junction of Graingers Lane and Corngreaves Road, Cradley Heath, *c.* 1900. This local inn was run for many years by the Cole family. One member of the family, Joe (see page 71), ran the leather-working side of the business, the window of which can be seen on the right-hand side of the building. (*Collection of Peter Barnsley*)

A determined-looking group of regulars posing outside the Sportsman pub, Old Hill, near the railway station (at one time it was probably called the Sportsman and Railway), which in common with many of the local pubs has in the past few years been renamed. It is now known as The Wharf (shades of Holt Fleet). It is interesting to note the number of caps and watch-chains being worn. (*Collection of Anthony H. Page*)

The Corngreaves Hotel in its final form, early 1970s. It was built opposite the large industrial complex that was once the site of the New British Iron Company's Corngreaves ironworks. This was wound up in 1893 and since its closure the site has become the home of many different trades and skills. The hotel itself has recently been demolished. (*Ron Moss*)

Spring Meadow House in Halesowen Road, Old Hill, early 1970s. This was one of the 'thirst quenchers' for the many manual workers in the area. Today it has been renamed the Spring Meadow and the brewery name changed to Banks's. The butchers shop on the corner of the road into Spring Meadow has been demolished and the shop of A.B. Jones now bears the name of DBR Cut Price & News. (*Ron Moss*)

Hand of Providence. This neat pub situated in Hollybush Street, most of which vanished under the clearance and rebuilding that took place in the mid-1970s, already has its windows covered and is awaiting the bulldozer in January 1973. A datestone, just visible to the right of the right upper window, surprisingly contained the information 'Park Street, 1851' and was saved after demolition by the son of one of the last landlords, John Broadhurst. In the past the landlords were the Prices (when a strong beer was brewed on the premises and the nickname 'Poshes' allegedly came about), Ernie and Vi Lloyd from around 1929 until 1937, and then Mr Broadhurst who took over until he retired in 1985. The pub was demolished shortly after this photograph was taken. (*Ron Moss*)

The Bell. This local hostelry, situated in St Anne's Road, just off the Five Ways, Cradley Heath, has a long distinguished history. Many interesting tales have been recorded during the time when mine host was the famous Benny Fiddler. After a few name changes it was decided to close its doors as a public house and it has recently been converted to living accommodation. (*Ron Moss*)

Halesowen Road, Old Hill, looking towards Netherton where industrial buildings can still be seen on the skyline. The well-known Castle Inn was demolished in the early months of 2001 and has been replaced by housing. The terrace alongside was demolished a few years earlier and has also been replaced by a modern housing development. (*Ron Moss*)

The Heath Tavern, High Street, Cradley Heath. This pub on the corner of Bank Street, in common with many local pubs, was very rarely referred to by its correct name. It was known to people over a wide area as the Bosta. This photograph, taken in about 1918 outside the Plant's pub, shows a charabanc party ready to move off on a trip. Although it stood empty for many years it was not finally demolished until September 1998. (*Collection of Karl Taylor*)

Opposite: The Gate Hangs Well, Halesowen Road, Old Hill. This pub, probably named after a toll-gate that controlled the traffic at a nearby road junction, was empty for a while, but in the mid-1990s it was demolished and replaced by houses. However, the left-hand brick-built gatepost leading to the yard at the rear is still in position together with the houses to the left of it. (*Ron Moss*)

The Railway pub in May 1970, when it was closed and its name signs were painted over. Situated just off the Five Ways, Cradley Heath, towards Lomey Town (Lower High Street) below Christ Church, this was one of the many pubs in the town that catered for the workers' thirsts. Mine host in the 1970s was a Mr Bennett. (*Ron Moss*)

The Royal Oak, 26 April 1959. This fairly large ancient pub in Lomey Town has over the years satisfied the thirsts of many chainmakers who toiled in the vicinity. Note the tie-bars around the building to protect it from mining subsidence; it looks as if some of the cottages above have already sunk a little. (*Ron Moss*)

4

Industry

The Black Country area was the home of a great many iron foundries and drop forging firms. In 1830 the Black Country had 123 blast furnaces producing pig-iron. This was the greatest number of blast furnaces in any iron-producing district at that time in the British Isles. In 1856, at its peak of production, the Black Country area made 777,000 tons of pig-iron. It then had 200 blast furnaces although only 110 were recorded as in blast. Cast-iron drainage goods from the area can be seen along many roads around the world, from Malta to small ports in Portugal. The name of 'Cradley Heath' is cast into many products used along roads that you may stroll along while on holiday both in the British Isles and abroad. Most of these foundries have been closed and their buildings demolished and replaced, in many instances, by housing. Here is just one example from our area, the firm of Dudley & Dowell Ltd; there are many more. (*Ron Moss*)

The iron foundry of Dudley & Dowell is very prominent here. Drain and manhole covers were cast in black sand and there is hardly a town or city in the world that did not use them. This photograph is taken in the old county of Staffordshire while the row of poplar trees which can be seen right centre, alongside St John's church, Dudley Wood, are situated in Worcestershire. Today the Mousesweet Brook at the bottom of the hill divides the MBCs of Sandwell and Dudley. In this area stood the ancient hamlet of Scolding Green, which has records running back to at least the sixteenth century. Two of its houses can still be seen next to the tall tree in the centre and featured in an episode of *Crossroads* two years later. They were demolished in May 1977. A new housing development now covers this area and efforts to keep the name of Scolding Green alive fell on deaf ears at the Sandwell HQ. (*John Pizzey*)

The change from foundry to flats. The site of the Dudley & Dowell Ltd foundry in 2003; the lampposts still occupy the same position, a good feature when comparing photographs. The chain pattern thoughtfully worked into the surrounding wall is a reminder of another of Cradley Heath's famous cable-chain manufacturers sited to the rear of the foundry site, Joseph Westwood. (*Ron Moss*)

Compton Road, Cradley Heath, at its junction with St Anne's Road (formerly Scolding Green Road) in 1971. Although the houses in the centre middle distance are still there the buildings on the two near corners have changed dramatically. Wendy's Café on the left has been replaced by modern flats, while the sand-casting iron foundry of Dudley & Dowell on the right was swept away some time ago and has recently also been replaced by a new housing development. (*John Pizzey*)

Corngreaves works entrance, early 1970s. The works weighbridge occupies the centre of this photograph, although it has since deteriorated and been demolished together with the remaining large chimney stack which formed the centre of the site long after it had served its purpose. The metre-gauge works railway left the works at this point, crossed the road and occupied the strip of land shown in the foreground alongside the Corngreaves Hotel before passing under the ex-GWR main line railway that connected Stourbridge to Birmingham and making its way to the canal basins sited on the Dudley No. 2 canal. (*Ron Moss*)

Joseph Penn's ironworks occupied the corner created by Providence Street and Newtown Lane, Cradley Heath, an area that 120 years previously had been the site of Noah Hingley's early works before he moved up to Netherton and created his well-known iron empire in 1837. This 1971 photograph shows Penn's No. 2 entrance in Newtown Lane, sandwiched between old Victorian housing stock before their demolition. (*John Pizzey*)

View from Lench's grounds, showing exactly how industrial the Old Hill area once was, *c.* 1920. The photograph is taken from the hill overlooking what was eventually to become the Powke Lane cemetery, from near T.W. Lench's Blackheath works at Ross. It appears that the cenotaph has just been erected and the paths are being laid. Almost in the centre can be seen the two blast furnaces and attendant ironworks on both sides of Powke Lane that were operated by Noah Hingley of Netherton. This is a very rare view of one of the many ironworks in the Black Country. Between the blast furnaces and the First World War field gun can be seen the Old Hill gasworks, with just a glimpse of the Dudley No. 2 canal to its left. Just to the left of the cenotaph is the hole in the ground where Messrs Partridge & Guest obtained the clay to make their bricks, with the brickyard buildings and engine house behind it. This hole was gradually filled in and now provides the site for the funfair and circus when they visit the area. (*Collection of Anthony H. Page*)

Opposite: Although this fine action photograph was taken at the London works, Barlow's Ltd, in 1936, it is typical of the rolling mills operated by Joseph Penn in his ironworks in the district. The steam is created by the water that is fed on to the rolls to keep them cool. (*M. Wyatt*)

Brickworks at the bottom of Barrs Road, 1970. This long continuous Hoffmann kiln was located on the old Congreaves ironworks site and probably turned out thousands of common house bricks. These were used to build the rows of workers' houses and workshops in the surrounding district. (*Ron Moss*)

Brickyard scene, *c.* 1972. Having a well-earned rest and a smoke is George Biddlestone. He is sitting on a typical brickyard barrow, of a design that has probably been used for hundreds of years in the brickyard at Corngreaves. A round kiln can be seen behind him, while in the background towers the large chimney-stack of the former New British Ironworks. (*Peter Barnsley*)

The entrance to the works of Doulton & Company, Doulton Road (between Old Hill and Rowley), 1969. This company was world famous for their glazed sanitary ware and pipes, examples of which can be found in almost every country worldwide. Most of the fireclay, which formed the body of their products, was transported by canal boat from the deep quarry excavated in the Saltwells coppice. (*John Pizzey*)

Down draught kiln awaiting demolition, 1969. This is an example of one of the many round kilns that were to be found in the works yard of Doulton's. The presence of suitable fireclay nearby as well as coal virtually beneath their feet to feed the kiln fires were the reasons for establishing this works in 1848. (*John Pizzey*)

This larger, oblong kiln, just before its demolition in 1969, was used by Doulton's to fire their sanitary pipes, judging by the broken examples on the left-hand side of the kiln entrance. The presence of piping around the sides of the kiln indicates that Doulton's had at some time converted this kiln from coal to oil burning. Quite often the oil used was waste sump oil that was drained from cars when they were serviced. (*John Pizzey*)

Car and bicycle parts. A pair of immaculately turned out pantechnicons belonging to a firm based on the Waterfall Lane Trading Estate that produced a myriad of parts for the motor and bicycle trade, such as lamps, wing mirrors and any other spare part that was required to keep wheeled vehicles on the road. Raydyot was established in 1849 and was a large employer in the district. (*Dunn's Imaging Group PLC*)

In 1908 Joe Cole's father married and moved a hundred yards or so up Grainger's Lane from the hotel and carried on Cole's leather business from there. Joe junior was born there in 1911. Joe later took over the family leather business and kept himself busy replacing and repairing the harness and tackle for 150 pit ponies. As the local collieries closed one by one the need for pit ponies gradually decreased, and by 1964 Joe realised that to make a living wage he must get a full-time job. He found himself, together with many other Black Country men, working at the giant Austin Motor Company at Longbridge, maintaining the leather fittings which were part of the hoists that moved the car bodies along the lines. On Saturdays he could still be found using his leather-working skills to carry out various repairs in his Grainger's Lane shop. (*Peter Barnsley*)

Joe Cole at work in his shop in Grainger's Lane, Cradley Heath, July 1972. His saddlery business was first established in 1890 when Joe Cole's grandfather was the licensee of the Corngreaves Hotel in Grainger's Lane. Joe's grandfather and one of his sons, who was Joe's father, ran the leather-working business from one of the rooms of the hotel. At that time the work of maintaining saddles and harnesses kept the family business going. (*Peter Barnsley*)

'Shakespeare's forgings'. The scene at the junction of Cox's Lane (looking down) and Powke Lane, 1969. The works of Joseph Shakespeare & Company Ltd, well known for its forgings, and the long-established White Lion Inn on the corner look smart and neat in this sunny morning view spoilt only by the weeds surrounding the postbox. The 'Gaffer's' Daimler is parked off the road outside the offices that would later be replaced by a larger more modern building set across the track of the Old Hill to Dudley railway branch line which had closed the previous year, a victim of the Dr Beeching purge. The solid building of the White Lion, although closed as an inn many years ago, has now found a new use as a café supplying the refreshment needs of the workers in the surrounding area. (*John Pizzey*)

An oliver-shop is a workshop where oliver hammers were used to forge oddwork (shelf brackets, rainwater goods, holding pipes, shackles, swivels and hooks). Olivers were also used in the early nailmaking industry. Treadle-operated versions can be traced back to 1352. An oliver set was still being used to make shackle pins at Wellings Forgings, Old Hill in 2000. The origin of the name is somewhat of a mystery. The best version that I have heard is from the story of Roland, the legendary nephew of the Emperor Charlemagne, whose constant companion knight was a large man named Oliver. When they went into battle he would protect and deliver blows for Roland. That is why a blacksmith is glad of the assistance of an oliver at the forge.

BLACKER'S PATENT

DOUBLE-HEADED

POWER "OLIVER" HAMMER.

NEW PATTERN, D.H TYPE.

THE ONLY
TOOL
OF ITS KIND
IN
THE WHOLE
WORLD.

PATENTED
IN ALL
COUNTRIES
AND
ENTIRELY
BRITISH.

This Hammer is invaluable to "Oliver" Workers, being in effect an "Oliver" Hammer arranged for belt drive.

The machine is driven by fast and loose pulleys, and is fitted with jingler blocks.

Less than one H.P. will drive, and the running cost is therefore remarkably small.

Many variations of this machine are made for special jobs and it is advisable to specify the work when seeking prices.

For single process jobs we offer a single headed variation of the above.

Except for Dies, the machine as supplied is complete ready for working.

Speed, 420 Revs.   Pulleys 15 in. dia. (for 2½ Belt).

BLACKER Limited,

STAYLEY IRONWORKS, STALYBRIDGE.

Telephone: 708 Ashton-under-Lyne.   Telegrams: "BLACKER," Stalybridge.

Opposite: The Clyde Street works of H.F. Shaw Ltd, 1971. As mentioned on the sign, one of their products was ships' tackle. This and other oddwork was produced in an 'oliver-shop' which can be seen on the other side of the gated yard entrance, the third building up on the left. The works was mentioned recently in the excellent booklet entitled *Dr Shaw Remembers.* This is taken from the very interesting diary of George Harold Shaw whose mother was Alice Cockin, an adopted daughter of George Alfred Haden-Best who lived in the new Haden Hill House. Dr Shaw's diary tells us that his father, John Edwin Shaw, married Miss Alice Cockin and they then moved into the old Haden Hall where he was born. Although his father trained as a teacher he decided to run his brother's manufacturing business in Clyde Street. He also became involved in local politics and received an OBE. H.F. Shaw Ltd, of Burton Road, Dudley, finally ceased trading in May 2003. (*John Pizzey*)

The oliver-shop of the Clyde Street works of H.F. Shaw Ltd being demolished on 7 April 1973. Two pairs of 'oliver stumps' can clearly be seen as well as the remains of the hearths where the metal was heated before being forged into shape. Note also the barred window openings looking out on to Clyde Street and also the provision for sliding shutters. (*Ron Moss*)

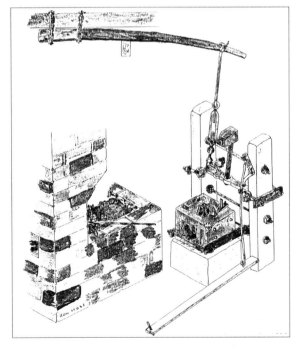

A nailmaker's hearth and oliver
(*Ron Moss*)

5

Chainmaking

Women chainmakers. This dramatic drawing captures the scene of women working hard in a Cradley Heath chainshop. It was published in a daily newspaper in 1971 and the original artwork is held by the National Museum of Labour History in Manchester. The nearest woman appears to be cutting her bar of iron in two after balancing it on the anvil to find the centre. This made it easier to work in the hearth because the women made their small chain directly from the bar. (Reproduced by permission of the archivist, National Museum of Labour History, Stephen Bird)

In the nineteenth and well into the twentieth century Cradley Heath and its surrounding area was world famous for its fine handmade chain that was manufactured from wrought iron. However, the supply of wrought iron dried up in the mid-1970s and the local chain trade finished in the winter of 1976.

The women who formed a substantial part of this industry manufactured the smaller sizes of chain from not much larger than watch chain to about $1\frac{1}{32}$in in diameter, this being the size of the bar that the chain was made from. The census of 1841 records that about forty-four women were engaged in chainmaking in the Staffordshire and Worcestershire area that makes up the Black Country; this had risen to 2,103 by 1911.

During the First World War, when army units required a great amount of chain to equip the many horses and wagons used, chainmakers worked flat out to satisfy the demand. After the war, with the greater use of lorries, the availability of cleaner, better paid employment and the development of electrically welded small chain, the numbers of small chainmakers declined. However, trade picked up in the Second World War with many workers forging chain in their backyard brewhouse chainshops. They finally laid down their hammers in the 1950s.

Lucy Woodhall, née Swingler. As the name Swingler is pencilled on the reverse of this portrait it was probably taken before Lucy married Jack Woodhall in Old Hill church in 1927. (*Peter Barnsley*)

Lucy Woodhall making chain at her hearth at Samuel Woodhouse & Sons Ltd in 1972, about a year before she retired – after making chain for sixty years and one month. (*Pete Barnsley*)

A typical 1920s studio photograph of Lucy together with probably her elder sister Alice, in the centre, and her great friend Annie Partridge on the right. Her son Trevor remembers taking his mother to Annie's Golden Wedding party at the Stone Manor Hotel many years ago. (*Trevor Woodhall*)

An outworker's family chainshop, St Lukes Street (originally Church Street), January 1973.
The small four- or five-hearth chainshop was once a common sight in the streets of the Black
Country chainmaking district. Several members of a family would work together to make the
small sizes of chain using rods of iron supplied by the chainmaster, who sometimes delivered
the rods and then collected the finished chain, often using a horse and cart. (*Ron Moss*)

Back garden chainshop, March/April 1974. This chainshop, actually in the back garden of a
house in Newtown Lane, is viewed from St Lukes Street, which connects Newtown Lane with
Meredith Street, Cradley Heath, and is within hours of demolition. The remains of the privy
can be seen to the right. During its later working years this shop was used by sisters who
made small chain to earn their living. (*Ron Moss*)

Allbut Street area, May 1973. This scene of demolition, in an area between Cradley Heath and Old Hill, gives a good idea of the typical mix of mid- to late nineteenth-century housing and small chainshops, together with the necessary brewhouses and toilets. (*Ron Moss*)

Bannister Street, Cradley Heath. This neat five-hearth chainshop has so far escaped the bulldozer. Its owner has even preserved a hearth and tommy hammer immediately on the right just inside the stable door. The barred window-frame openings have been replaced by conventional glazed windows so that part of the shop can be used as a store. A pulley can be seen over the door to facilitate the loading of chain on to a cart. (*Ron Moss*)

Oak Street, Old Hill. This range of chainshops had their doorways at a height that was more convenient for the loading of goods on to carts or wagons than for use by workers. When photographed in 1971 the offices on the left were used by Mainline Products (Richards) Ltd. Park Street can just be seen on the extreme left. (*John Pizzey*)

A group of Cradley Heath chainmakers, *c.* 1930; most are still wearing their aprons (made of canvas or leather). The only person identified so far is Joe Price, who is sitting in the front row to the right of the 'Moses basket' or swill. These baskets were used to carry the fuel, known as the breeze (small washed coke), to the chainmakers' hearths. (*Ron Griffiths*)

Opposite: Newtown Lane, Cradley Heath, 1971. This small but smart terracotta-decorated single-storey building, which once stood opposite School Street, was the office of one of the many chainmaking firms in the Cradley Heath and Old Hill area. The firm was founded in about 1860 by Emmanuel Woodhouse who was joined by his sons Albert and Caleb, the firm later adopting the name of Woodhouse Brothers. They moved to these larger premises, located on the corner of Newtown Lane and Providence Street, during the First World War to enable them to manufacture the larger 4-inch diameter chain. (*John Pizzey*)

The Cradley Heath district was world famous for its fine quality chain. In this December 1975 photograph, a couple of years before the handmade chain trade ended, Clarrie Johnson is 'scarfing' the link before 'shutting' it, the tapered side of the hammer being used. (*Ron Moss*)

Clarrie is now finishing off the shut link by 'tommying' it. He is bringing the top tool of the treadle-operated tommy hammer down on to the link to bring the join back to its original diameter which looks to be around ⅞in. One can tell this cable chain is completely made by hand by the beautiful symmetrical shape that has been achieved. (*Ron Moss*)

Chain test shop. Chain that is required to serve an important purpose, especially that of anchoring large ships, needs to be tensile-tested to a load according to its diameter that is specified by Lloyds of London. On the left a gentleman is inspecting lengths of chain that have just been tested in the test bed, while on the right can be seen lengths of cable chain which have been dipped in a large vat of a bitumen-type product to help keep out the corrosive effects of seawater. (*Ron Moss*)

Integral stud chain. This finished length of fairly large cable chain is made up of links that during their manufacture have had the centre stud or stay-pin forged on the bar before bending, so that the stud is an integral part of the outer part. The join can just be seen below the stud on each link. This is the type of chain needed by a ship that has to ride out vicious storms. Another piece of chain can be seen in the iron channel of the test bed. (*Ron Moss*)

Oyster 'nets'. While researching the Cradley Heath chain trade over the past thirty years I have photographed chainmakers forging chain and parts for fishing gear for trawlers, but I was quite surprised in 2002 when, at a lecture, a member of my audience produced two well-worn photographs of her late father and her two aunts who manufactured oyster nets in a forge in Old Field works, Corngreaves, Cradley Heath. This photograph, from about 1910, shows Joseph Morris and his two sisters with the oyster net they have just made spread out in front of them. (*Mrs J.E. Humphries*)

6

Religious Buildings & Groups

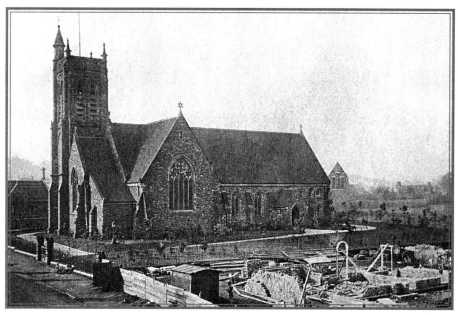

Holy Trinity church, Old Hill, *c.* 1900. In the foreground construction has just started on the Old Hill Police Station and Magistrates Court. Immediately behind the church is possibly a glimpse of the Rowley Regis Board offices, demolished some years ago. To its right can be seen some old cottages in Lawrence Lane. This photograph was probably taken from the bridge of the New British Iron Company's Congreaves railway that crossed the Halesowen Road at this point. (*BCS Collection*)

Christ Church, Five Ways, Cradley Heath: a rare photograph of the inside of Christ Church, viewed from the balcony and showing the organist at practice. The date is not known but it is probably before the Second World War. (*J.M. McKay*)

Foundation stones being laid at the Whitley Memorial Sunday School located opposite the junction of Foxoak Street and St Anne's Road, Cradley Heath. Mr Simeon Homer (hatless with his back to the camera) can be seen laying one of the stones. After its duty as a religious building was over it was used for several other purposes. This Sunday school might well have had a new front added later as the present frontage cannot be married to that seen in the photograph. There is also a distinct difference between the bricks used in the frontage and the older ones used on the rear of the building. Today no foundation stones are evident on the front of the building. Above the entrance the date '1910' has been moulded in buff terracotta. The foundation stone can be seen on the inner wall as you enter the Sunday school. (*Collection of Anthony H. Page*)

Male voice choir. A 1935 group photograph of the Cradley Heath and Old Hill Male Voice Choir, photographed on the grassed area to the rear of the Whitley Memorial Sunday School in Cradley Heath. (*Anthony H. Page*)

Whitley Sunday School teachers. Both of these photographs are of Whitley Memorial Sunday School teacher groups, probably taken on the grassed area to the rear of the Sunday school. There is no date, but the dress indicates that it is sometime in the 1930s. The names of the teachers present are not known. It is interesting to note the buildings in the background; could they be the brewhouse and toilet of the dwelling next door? (*J. McKay*)

A church outing to a local beauty spot from Cradley Heath Christ Church, July 1934. The following participants are known: the couple standing in the centre of the back row are Gwen and Norman Viner. Front row, left to right: Ernest Fellows, Alfred Smith, Rhoda McKay, -?-, Basil Hingley. (*J. McKay*)

Out in the country. Members of the Cradley Heath Christ Church Young People's Society on a ramble to the Walton Hills on 3 September 1932. Photograph taken by Billy Goode. (*J. McKay*)

Whitley Memorial Sunday School teachers, 1930. Quite a few of the teachers' names have been recalled and many will be familiar to Cradley Heath people. Back row, left to right: Norman Viner, Basil Hingley, Jack Hartland, Alf Price, P. Austin, Reg Adams, -?-, -?-, Vernon Richards. Third row: Percy Fellows, Ben White, Ernest Fellows, -?-, -?-, Ivy Pitchford, -?-, Billy Goode, Sam White, Nellie Johnson, Elsie Viner, Edna Kilvert, Rhoda Fellows, Rene Kilvert, Nora Rock. Second row: -?-, Gladys Davies, -?-, Grace Roberts, Ivy Noons,? Hetheridge, -?-, Dora Flemming, Polly White, Marion Deeley, Clarice Biggs, -?-, Nellie Viner, Dora Bradley. Seated: Dolly Viner, Margaret Fellows, Mr Kendrick, Revd Thomas McKay, Alfred Smith, Gideon Smith, Phyllis McKay. (*J. McKay*)

Opposite: The interior of Christ Church, Five Ways, Cradley Heath, on the occasion of the 1932 Harvest Festival. (*J. McKay*)

Kinver outing. This photograph comes from a collection labelled 'Christ Church outings'. A good indication of the location is the unusual building sited on the hillside, above the shoulder of the gentleman on the right. A similar photograph featured in the book *Drakelow Unearthed*, the story of the wartime factory under Kinver Edge, shows the same building. Apparently the local ironmaster, William Hancox of Blakeshall Hall, created a Swiss-style village and this building was a school and later a mission where occasional church services were held up to at least 1921. (*J. McKay*)

Boy Scouts of the 1st Cradley Heath troop, St Luke's, taking part in a camp, *c.* 1943–4. Seated in front is Scoutmaster William (Bill) Page. Standing, left to right: Ray Knowles, Harry Darby, -?-, Ronnie Bate, Ken Moss, Ronnie Moss, Alan Priest, Jack Bennett. (*Collection of Ron Moss*)

7

Processions & Parades

The civic dignitaries of Warley turned out to march with the band at the head of the procession along Halesowen Road through the centre of Old Hill. Councillor Tromans is in front, with Joe Adams and his wife in the second row and the band following behind, passing what was for a hundred years the unchanged row of shops that made up the one side of Old Hill town. (*Ron Moss*)

The young drummers
of the band in their
uniforms take their
time from their drum
major. The residents of
Old Hill made sure that
they received a warm
welcome. (*Ron Moss*)

Warley Music Festival, July 1972. The old Borough of Warley used to arrange these special events. On this occasion the council invited over the Swiss Marching Band known as *Knabenmusik Kreuzlingen*, seen here in their national dress, with their flags proudly flying. (*Ron Moss*)

Sunday School Treat Day, 3 July 1937. The banner reads GOD SO LOVED THE WORLD and lower down METHODIST SUNDAY SCHOOL, REDDAL HILL. This outdoor service, supported by the Cradley Heath Salvation Army Band, is taking place in Plant Street, Old Hill. The Grade II listed library can be seen in the background. The service is being taken by the Revd J.J. Cook. The Corngreaves Infant School, built by the British Iron Company of Corngreaves for the education of their workers' children, just creeps into the picture on the left. (*Jack Porter*)

Opposite: Cradley Heath Salvation Army Band returning to their barracks in Newtown Lane via School Street, after they had provided the music for St Luke's Sunday School 'treat and parade', *c.* 1931. The school, which is still in regular use, can be seen in the background. (*Ron Griffiths*)

Rowley Regis Charter parade, 28 September 1933. As part of the celebration of the incorporation of the Borough of Rowley Regis Charter, the Band of The Scots Guards under the command of Lt H.E. Dowel parade along High Street, Blackheath, heading towards Old Hill. The long-established shop of B. Hobbs, unfortunately no longer there today, can be seen on the left. (*Sandwell Archives, Smethwick*)

Rowley Regis Charter celebrations. A huge crowd (mostly men) gather around the makeshift stage in Temple Meadow, Old Hill, to witness the ceremony of the incorporation of the Borough of Rowley Regis Charter. The site can be located today by the row of detached houses in the background which are almost at the top of the hill in Halesowen Road, opposite the gates of Haden Hill Park. Just over four years later, on 23 October 1937, on this very spot, Alderman Thomas Deeley, Mayor of Rowley Regis, laid the foundation stone of the offices of the Rowley Regis Borough Council, known later as the Municipal Buildings, situated in Barrs Road. This splendid building was opened on 17 December 1938 by Mr Joseph Eley. The contractors were J.M. Tate & Sons. (*Sandwell Archives, Smethwick*)

Rowley Regis Charter in Temple Meadow. A close-up of the platform in Temple Meadow, with the Rt Hon. George Lansbury addressing the assembled crowd with the Charter Clerk Mr Clifford Buckley (in the bowler hat to the left) and the other civic dignitaries present at the ceremony. (*Sandwell Archives, Smethwick*)

The Cradley Heath Salvation Army Band passing down Highgate Street, on their return to the barracks after taking part in a parade in the early 1970s. Foster's wine shop and 'Outdoor' in the background was formerly the Beehive pub. A large traffic island serving the Old Hill bypass now occupies its site. There are at least two women members of the band but on seeing the photographer they have cleverly hidden themselves behind the men. (*Ron Moss*)

The children and Sunday school teachers line up for the start of the Anniversary Parade in Greenfield Avenue, Lomey Town, Cradley Heath, late 1930s. They will probably make their way towards the Whitley Memorial Sunday School or Christ Church, Five Ways, for a service and a 'treat'. More houses were built on the left-hand side of the avenue after the Second World War. (*J. McKay*)

The four photographs on pages 102–3, loaned by Ms *J. McKay*, show the preparation that went into Sunday school or anniversary parades. Here, the children are being organised into a parade with the decorated, highly polished lorry (Morris Commercial?) supplied by Palmers Milk (Cradley Heath) Ltd. (*J. McKay*)

Above and opposite below: The location of these photographs is at the end of Foxoak Street opposite the Whitley Memorial School building. Apparently the large tall building on the right of the photographs, long gone, was an Admiralty Stores where products for the Royal Navy, such as chains, anchors, shackles and so on that were all manufactured in the district, were stored awaiting despatch. This area has been used for many years as Cradley Heath's main shoppers' car park. (*J. McKay*)

Another view of the parade being organised also shows, in the background, the gable-end of an old workshop which is still there today. This is situated on the opposite side to the Admiralty Stores on Foxoak Street. (*J. McKay*)

These very rare photographs, probably taken with a family-owned Brownie box camera, show street parties that were organised to celebrate the coronation of King George VI and Queen Elizabeth (the late Queen Mother) in 1937. They were all taken in Best Street, Old Hill. (*The Collection of the late Mrs Dorothy Andrews of Dudley Wood Road*)

This photograph is taken looking up Best Street towards High Street (later Highgate Street). (*The Collection of the late Mrs Dorothy Andrews of Dudley Wood Road*)

The view down Best Street looking towards Cox's Lane. (*The Collection of the late Mrs Dorothy Andrews of Dudley Wood Road*)

The view towards the High Street. (*The Collection of the late Mrs Dorothy Andrews of Dudley Wood Road*)

'Rhubarb Chapel' anniversary parade. The anniversary parade or 'walk-about' was quite a regular occurrence until the 1980s but has since faded away; perhaps the roads are now too dangerous. Here are two views of the parade from St James's Wesleyan Reform church, located on Old Hill Cross, c. 1965. The above picture shows the parade of children and helpers turning into Highgate Street (formerly High Street) from Halesowen Road. The two ladies have gained a good vantage point by climbing out of the upstairs window of Sidaway's wallpaper shop. (*Ron Moss*)

Carnival parade. These parades were a regular feature of local life in the area in the 1920s and '30s. Here, a parade is passing through Reddal Hill led by a jazz band from Old Hill; crowds of sightseers line the route. The shop behind the banner, with the extended shade, is now occupied by Ivan's fish and chip shop and restaurant. The next two shops were occupied by the French family and the area was known locally as 'French's Corner'. Some shops are still used for business while some are purely residential. Note the tracks in the road used by the trams from Cradley Heath to Dudley; this service ended on 31 December 1929. (*Collection of Anthony H. Page*)

Opposite: Here part of the parade can be seen passing the infants school next to Old Hill parish church and Lawrence Lane. (*Ron Moss*)

A Remembrance Day parade emerging from Spring Meadow in the late 1970s to join the Halesowen Road on its way to the cenotaph in Powke Lane cemetery, via Old Hill Cross. The members of the parade have probably assembled at the British Legion Club in Spring Meadow. Behind the flag-bearer (the pole of which appears to have been used as a vertical focal point by the photographer, giving the Spring Meadow tavern in the background a leaning appearance) can be seen Peter Archer MP (later Lord Archer). (*Collection of Anthony H. Page*)

8

Sports & Leisure

1962–3 crib league winners. The Hand of Providence pub, situated in Holly Bush Street, Cradley Heath, was well known for its cribbage team. This photograph was taken when they were the league winners for the 1962–3 season. The members whose names have been recalled are, standing back row, left to right: Cyril Broadhurst, licensee of the Hand of Providence, -?-, Jess Tromans, John Broadhurst (licensee's son), Joe Bate, -?-, -?-. On the front row seated only two people can be identified: the first gentleman on the left was once a barman at the Manchester (the Four Ways Inn), and the third man from the left is Bert Deeley; perhaps someone might recall the remainder. (*Collection of John Broadhurst*)

The Blackcountryman's love of pigeons is well known throughout the world. Here we see a Pigeon Club meeting at the Blue Ball Inn, Bearmore Road, Old Hill, in March 1964. (*MBSC Smethwick Archives*)

Haden Hill Swimming Baths seen unused and derelict in 1972. Hundreds, maybe thousands, of children who attended schools in Cradley Heath and Old Hill are grateful for the swimming lessons that they received in these outdoor baths in Haden Hill Park. As can be seen, they were within sight of the Old Tudor hall and the newer Haden Hill House, both of which have been recently restored. A centenary celebration booklet published in 1977 by Old Hill Primary School recounts that 'close connection between physical education and medicine was strengthened and outdoor pursuits encouraged, with the school giving their first swimming lesson at Haden Hill Park Baths on 7 July 1927'. The records for Macefield School in Old Hill recall that 'Swimming was first taught in 1940–1 when Haden Hall Open Air Swimming pool was used for lessons.' In the 1950s lessons were transferred to Smethwick. The site of the baths is now used as a car park. (*M. Wyatt*)

Opposite: 'They're off': one of the Blackcountryman's hobbies is his love of dogs and this photograph shows the start of a heat of whippet racing. The 'spectator' dogs also enjoy it. (*Ron Moss*)

'The Heathens': a marvellous record of the Cradley Heath Speedway team's first ever Rider Parade around the cinder track on 21 June 1947. Leading the team from left to right are: Ray Beaumont, Les Beaumont, Alan Hunt, Phil Malpass, Eric Irons, Geoff Bennett, Stan Crouch, Jimmy Wright. These names will never be forgotten in the history of speedway racing at Cradley Heath. Note the rough beginnings of the surrounding fencing and the non-paying spectators who are peering over it. (*Collection of Peter Foster*)

Alan Hunt will always be remembered as one of the pioneers of this exciting sport at the Dudley Wood track that drew larger and larger crowds to the stadium. (*Collection of Peter Foster*)

Geoff Bennett can always be guaranteed to produce a smile. Here he is in 1947. Little wonder that all the crowd roared out 'Hommer 'um Crerdley' as our lads roared over the winning line. (*Collection of Peter Foster*)

This 1948 team photo includes a good illustration of one of the high-powered bikes, which had no brakes, that thrilled the crowds and showered them with black cinders, if you happened to be in the right spot on the corner of the track. The team from left to right are Eric Irons, Bill Clifton, Gil Craven, Les Beaumont, Ray Beaumont, Phil Malpass, Alan Hunt (kneeling). (*Collection of Peter Foster*)

The Heathens team of 1949, in their original leathers. Standing, left to right: Les Beaumont, Jack Arnfield, Bill Clifton, Roy Moreton. Kneeling: Eric Williams, Alan Hunt, Phil Malpass, Gil Craven. (*Collection of Peter Foster*)

A mixture of old and new faces in the 1952 team. Standing, left to right: -?-, Wilf Wilstead, Guy Allott, Les Tolley, Harry Bastable, Brian Shepherd, and their mechanic Bill Sponcer. Kneeling: Derek Braithwaite, Fred Perkins, Phil Malpass, Jim Tolley. (*Collection of Peter Foster*)

The team after re-forming in 1960. After a short break, and with Phil Malpass as manager, the team consisted of, from left to right, Tony Eadon, Eric Eadon, George Bewley, Ronnie Rolf (seated on his machine), Phil Malpass (manager), Harry Bastable, Roy Spencer, Vic White. (*Collection of Peter Foster*)

9

Miscellany

The wringer. Here is a classic hand-operated wringer or mangle used to 'wring' as much water from the washing as possible before it was hung out on the line to dry. These models hardly changed for years and were an important part of the equipment in the 'brewus' at the back of the house. This one, having worked for many years, is on its way to the Black Country Museum in August 1973. (*Ron Moss*)

The Valeting CLOTHES CARE Service
AND SPEEDY LAUNDRY LTD

OUR REF. GF/MH

HEAD OFFICES & WORKS   PHONES: CRADLEY 6861 / 4

CRADLEY HEATH Staffs

BRANCHES THROUGHOUT THE MIDLANDS

YOUR REF.

Distinctive

DRY CLEANERS
AND DYERS

29th October, 1957.

The Valeting Service. There was hardly a family in the Old Hill, Cradley Heath, area that did not have a relative that either worked at or had been employed at The Valeting Service, located in the Newtown area right on the border between Worcestershire and Staffordshire. This was a prosperous laundry and dry cleaning company in the 1940s and '50s, ably managed by Mrs Marshall, with service shops in most of the surrounding towns. Their letterhead, reproduced above, proudly shows a RAF fighter plane to illustrate their speedy service to customers. Since the company closed down the substantial buildings, which are still there, have been used by several different firms for a variety of purposes.

Two groups of 'valeting girls' (left and opposite) photographed at the rear of the works in the mid-1950s. Back row, left to right: Sylvia Griffiths, Louie Billingham. Front row: -?-, Lily Cox.

Two of the same young women appear in both pictures but I have included them because they have as their background a clear view of what was known to locals as 'Scotsman's Hill'. This is a high vantage point from which spectators, who refrained from paying, could watch the speedway racing of the Cradley Heath 'Heathens' and their opponents in the Dudley Wood stadium.

Opening of the Workers' Institute. In 1910 women chainmakers were locked out of their workshops for refusing to work when their employees would not pay them the minimum wage that the Trade Board had agreed on, which was 2½d per hour. They were assisted by Miss Mary Macarthur, secretary of the Women's Trade Union League, who came up from London with other titled ladies to help the women in their fight. This dispute dragged on for around thirteen weeks until the employers agreed to pay them the minimum wage. After the struggle it was agreed that some of the funds that remained should be used to build a monument to the women's struggle. A piece of land was purchased on the corner of Lower High Street (Lomey Town) and Whitehall Road and this institute was built. One suggestion was that it could be used to teach the women workers of the district to write; it had been noticed that when the women came to sign on for their strike pay, many of them could only sign with a cross. This photograph shows the Countess of Dudley officially opening the Workers' Institute on 8 June 1912, at a ceremony held by the water fountain at the front of the building. (This does not work at present, but I have recently spoken to someone who can remember being refreshed by a drink from it.) It appears that most of the audience are women chainmakers in their glorious hats. It was on this site, once a 'pit-bonk', that many of the strike meetings were held. (*Sandwell Archives, Smethwick*)

The architect's impression of the Workers' Institute, Lomey Town (Lower High Street), Cradley Heath, which was originally to be called the Women Workers' Institute; below is the finished building. This is one of the historic buildings soon to be demolished to make way for the Cradley Heath bypass.

Corrugated buildings. Possibly because of their proximity to the famous Netherton ironworks of Noah Hingley, many buildings close to the works utilised the famous corrugated-iron sheeting that he boasted would never rust or rot away. Three of the local buildings around Darby End (or Derby Hand) lasted well into recent years. Here is one of the two shops in the area that provided a home and served the local populace with supplies for probably a hundred years. (*Ron Moss*)

Clark's Stores. This is the other corrugated-iron shop that once stood at the junction of Northfield Road and Cole Street, Darby End. It was demolished many years ago and replaced by a mini-superstore and a fish and chip establishment. (*Ron Moss*)

In the first book of *Cradley Heath, Old Hill & District*, published in 1998, the achievements of members of the local Jones family of Reddal Hill were related. John Jones founded several local shoe shops (one is still in business today) serving the local population. One of his sons, John Cooksey-Jones (he included his mother's surname in his), rose to the rank of brigadier in the Indian Army, while *his* son, Richard Stanton-Jones (like his father he included his mother's maiden name), became chief designer for the aircraft firm of Saunders-Roe at their Isle of Wight headquarters, where he worked on the SRN4 Hovercraft the Black Knight and other British missiles, and later helped to design supersonic fighters for the RAF. In this edition we again mention the achievements of a member of a family from Reddal Hill, one of whose descendants emigrated to Canada and became a bishop. Their history unfolds with the following photographs.

Phoebe Winwood, *c.* 1901. She was a nailer and, together with her husband Thomas, lived in Foxoak Street, Cradley Heath, in 1881. Thomas was a coalminer and he died in 1892 aged eighty-four. Phoebe had a busy life bringing up eleven children; she died in 1902. (*J. McKay*)

Phoebe and Albert Knock. Phoebe was the youngest daughter of Thomas and Phoebe Winwood. She married Albert, a chainmaker, on 5 September 1880 at St John's church, Dudley. Albert was the son of Levi Nock of the hamlet of Reddal Hill (between Old Hill and Cradley Heath) and his ancestry has been traced back to an entry in the records of St Giles' church, Rowley. The entry records the marriage in 1610 of William Knock and Ann Grove. After several house moves Phoebe and Albert finally settled in Whitehall Road, Cradley Heath. They had fourteen children of whom nine reached adulthood. (*J. McKay*)

Alice and Walter Jeavons-Fellows. Alice was the first child of Phoebe and Albert Knock. She married Walter, a chainmaker, and lived in the family home in Whitehall Road, Cradley Heath. Alice was the only child of the family to remain in Cradley Heath in her adult life. Four of the children emigrated to Canada and one to Australia, while the remaining three moved 'over the border' into Birmingham. Alice and Walter had three children. (*J. McKay*)

Ernest, Rhoda and Alice, the children of Alice and Walter Jeavons-Fellows, photographed in about 1920. Ernest married local girl Polly White, and Rhoda married Alexander McKay who was the son of the Revd Thomas McKay, Minister of Christ Church, Cradley Heath, from 1929 until 1932. Alice married Basil Johnson of Old Hill. (*J. McKay*)

Rt Revd Frank Foley-Nock and the Revd Peter A. McKay at a family reunion in Cradley on 7 August 1982. Frank Foley-Nock was Bishop of Algoma, Canada, from 1975 until shortly before his death in 1989. He was the great-grandson of Phoebe and Thomas Winwood, the grandson of Phoebe and Albert Knock and the son of Harry and Helen Knock (née Foley), both formerly of Cradley Heath. Peter McKay (on the left), a retired Methodist minister now residing in Buckinghamshire, is the son of Rhoda and Alexander McKay and the great-great-grandson of Phoebe and Thomas Winwood (see p. 121). (*J. McKay*)

The story of Haden Hall and Haden Hall Park, which on the demise of its last owner George Alfred Best MA on 6 October 1921 was put up for sale and purchased by the well-known local colliery proprietor Robert Fellows, formerly of Corngreaves Hall, who by this time was residing at Rudge Hall, Pattingham, is well documented. Not so well known is the fact that although the hall and park had been purchased by funds raised by local businessmen, then handed over to Rowley Regis Council on condition that they could be used by the general public forever from 21 October 1922, the local council actually proposed to demolish the hall in 1934. This was because it had not been occupied for over fifty years and its condition was becoming dangerous. Joseph Perry (shown above) and his brother the Revd Lyttleton Perry, both of whom had been involved with raising the funds for the original purchase back in 1921, again sprang into action by calling upon the local businessmen, including a relative of the Haden family, Mr A.M. Bassano, to raise the necessary funds to effect repairs to save the building. Mr J. Wilson Jones relates this story in his book *The History of the Black Country*, and refers to Joseph Perry as 'The Chainmaker Poet'. In a *County Express* newspaper article supplied by Jack Porter it is reported that Mr Perry, a lay preacher of Reddal Hill, had written many poems and also a book entitled *Palestine, the Enchanted Land*. He also made chain in a chainshop in Lawrence Lane, Old Hill. He was an avid reader and was apparently seen on many occasions reading while making chain. (*Jack Porter*)

No. 128 High Street (later Highgate Street). This small building bearing the date 1885 has served many purposes over the years. It is thought to have been built as a register office, which probably accounts for the fancy urn decoration on the façade. It later served as the Old Hill Labour Club up to 1920, when a piece of land was purchased (for £150) in nearby Halesowen Road and a new club building was constructed. It also served as the headquarters for the local Boy Scouts troop, a betting shop, and finished up with the rear quarters being used by John Sidaway for his painting and decorating business. This small historic building was demolished on 28 November 1986. Birch's cake shop to its left still exists and forms part of the Alachi International Restaurant, which offers its customers a white limousine service. (*Ron Moss*)

A leafy lane in Surrey maybe or perhaps Worcester or Sutton Coldfield? No, Compton Road where it meets up with Sydney Road in Cradley Heath. This beautiful building, sheltering in the right-hand corner among the trees, was Compton Grange, the home of local businessman Mr Tom Price. Sadly it was demolished not long after this photograph was taken in 1971 to make way for half a dozen houses that were built in its place. The fronts of these houses are located in Silverthorne Lane (which once contained the hamlet of Lomey Town, a similar industrial hamlet to Mushroom Green) and all that remains is one of the gate pillars. The gateway itself is bricked up. (*John Pizzey*)

Opposite: The original Corngreaves Hall was built by the famous ironmaster James Attwood in about 1780 and this is believed to have been on the site of a much earlier moated grange (a building date of which has been quoted as AD 800). Corngreaves Hall has been much altered, rebuilt and added to over the years. Many of the old industrialists liked to think that they lived in their own castles and the castellations around the roof-line served to give that effect. (*Ron Moss*)

This is how the grand entrance to the grounds of Corngreaves Hall appeared in January 1976. As it is wintertime and some of the trees have shed their leaves the hall appears quite clearly above the gateless entrance. Since then much restoration has been carried out here. (*Ron Moss*)

ACKNOWLEDGEMENTS

I am very grateful to the many people who have loaned photographs and provided information so that interesting, and, I hope, accurate information could be put into the captions that accompany the wide variety of photographs in this book. These help us to record some of the interesting events that have taken place in our area and, above all, form a lasting record of the many historic buildings that we have lost in the last few years in the Cradley Heath and Old Hill area.

My grateful thanks must go to Sandwell Community History & Archives Service, based at Smethwick Library, and Smethwick Photographic Society, whose members kindly deposited photographs in the Archives that show the history of the area. A particular great thank you must go to the late John Pizzey, who spent so much time recording the scenes of the area on many occasions in the 1970s accompanied by his son Frank, who I also thank for his help. Many of John's photographs are reproduced in the book.

I must pass on a big thank you to the following people whose photographs have enbled me to cover and illustrate a wide range of subjects dealing with the Cradley Heath and Old Hill area: Dorothy Andrews, Peter Barnsley, John Broadhurst, Dunn's Imaging Group PLC, Peter Foster, Geographers A–Z Map Co., Ltd, Ron Griffiths, Joyce McKay, Anthony H. Page, Jack Porter, Karl Taylor, Edith Tromans, Trevor Woodhall and M. Wyatt.

I must also pay tribute to the 'old' photographers who captured scenes in the district over the past 100 years – men such as, Bassano, Beech, Cockin, Everet, Forrest and Yelland, whose photographs turn up to delight us every now and again.